I0625549

RISK MANAGEMENT

FOR SMALL BUSINESSES

7 Effective Strategies to Understand,
Identify and Navigate Risks That
Will Make or Break Your Business

RHYS LI

Risk Management for Small Businesses
Li, Rhys
rhysli.co@gmail.com
www.rhysli.co

First Edition, June 2023

ISBN: 979-8-218-23509-3 (Paperback)

3

TABLE OF CONTENTS

IS THIS BOOK FOR YOU?

Are you a business owner or just starting out as an entrepreneur and you're faced with challenges in trying to
grow? Most of the time people see it as a lack of something
that prevents your business from flourishing. Based on
my experience as a risk consultant, what can hold businesses back is the lack of knowledge in identifying both,
operational and business risks. As a business owner are
you facing any of the following challenges:

- Are you concerned about protecting your
  bottom line?
- Have you ever experienced disruptions in your
  business?
- Do you feel the pressure to stay ahead of the
  competition?
- Are you finding it challenging to navigate legal
  complexities?
- Do you worry about creating a safe and happy
  workplace for your employees?
- Are you struggling to maximize your limited
  resources?

- Are you striving to build a strong foundation for growth?
- Do you want to cultivate a positive image for your business?
- Are you finding it challenging to strike a balance between your business responsibilities and spending quality time with your family?
- Are you concerned about providing financial stability for your family while also investing in your business?
- What steps have you taken to establish a succession plan?
- How do you take the potential consequences of your choices into account when making decisions?
- How are you managing family roles and expectations while maintaining clear boundaries and communication channels in your business?
- What contingency plans do you have in place to navigate through tough times?
- As a business owner, how do you take care of your physical and emotional health?

When it comes to identifying and prioritizing what you're trying to achieve, and how it might affect you, it is hard to see the full picture. In analyzing risk, we are looking at both the competition and opportunity for you and your business. I help design systems that allow you and your business to run at a higher level of achievement.

This book is for you if you are a have no risks background or want to make your business soundproof to sustain risks and grow. If you are an entrepreneur or a small business and would like to concentrate on growing your business, this book is for you as well. This book is to serve to educate you with *basic* risk knowledge.

For a deeper dive into your business, feel free to contact me via **rhysli.co@gmail.com** or visit **www.rhysli.co**.

Part I: Foundations for Growth

CHAPTER 1:
INTRODUCTION

Great businesses aren't just known for what they do — they're known for what they survive.

YOU'VE HEARD THE STATISTICS. Startups, small business owners, and entrepreneurs are walking hazards.

The infamous statistic estimates that 90% of all startups fail.

10% meet their fate in Year 1.

70% fail between Years 2-5, while the rest fade over time.

Despite the facts, entrepreneurs continue to make their mark. A 2018 Insureon poll reveals that 84% of small business owners label themselves "risk-takers." While many individuals opt for the safety and security of a W-2 and 9-5, entrepreneurs establish their businesses on the idea that the reward will outweigh the risk. Every day, founders are consciously and subconsciously performing risk assessments. It's basic psychology — it's built in our evolution and survival instincts to know when an action or inaction threatens our security.

In the investing world, we call this the *risk-reward spectrum*: the correlation between how much risk was involved in an investment and the returns received. In principle, the higher the risk, the higher the potential returns; but the higher the risk, the greater the potential losses will be.

Risk is often only discussed in a business's first year. Yet as we see, the majority of failed startups meet their fates between Years 2-5. This is often where businesses enter the *growth* stage. As the business develops, its needs grow more complex, and founders are required to make crucial decisions. From hiring team members to expanding their offerings, these decisions can either propel growth or sink the ship. Any decisions that allow growth are inherently risky. The risk-reward spectrum shows we can't grow without taking a risk. But with one miscalculated turn, and a rocky foundation, everything can crumble down in an instant.

Growing your business isn't just seeking opportunities and expanding your reach. It's reinforcing your foundation by spotting the cracks and vulnerabilities. It's defending what you've built so you can continue to build more. It's knowing the *worst* that could happen so you can plan and prepare for the *best*.

Great businesses aren't just known for what they *do* — they're known for what they *survive*. The growth trajectory of your business can be assessed by your level of resilience, and this starts at the foundation.

The Five Pillars of Risk Resilience

I am a Certified Organization and Leadership Coach. I've been a professional Risk Consultant since 2004, guiding and empowering international companies to manage their risks. Working as a risk consultant for over 20 years, I've discovered this risk resilience is built on five key pillars: *Communication, Strategic, Futuristic, Competition,* and *Deliberative.* I have served as a consultant for some of Fortune 500 companies.

Communication is the core tool we use to solve conflict, whether personal or professional. Your communication skills are either an asset or a liability to your business.

Strategic thinking is the *closest* skill humans have to predicting the future. Anyone can spot a risk, but not everyone can strategize a solution to avoid, escape, or resolve that risk. This is the very work I do as a risk consultant and strategist.

Developing a **futuristic** perspective is essential for growth. Growth is future-oriented; it requires us to acknowledge and plan that there's room for more. As we clarify our visions, it becomes easier to transform them into reality.

Competition is an inherent risk of entrepreneurship. Growth is just as much a defensive strategy as it is an offensive strategy. Identifying risks requires you to pinpoint where your business is in relation to the market and the top players in the industry.

Lastly, growth is **deliberative**. Often, entrepreneurs make the mistake of believing their business's success and failure are out of their control — that all risks and rewards are unexpected and a result of "luck." But deliberate risk analysis *creates* opportunities and options. It expects the unexpected and plans for the "what ifs' ' to put control back into your hands.

Any company can grow, but not every company can grow *sustainably*. Risk management is nearly synonymous with a business growth strategy. This is where we'll begin: As we map out your path toward growth, we'll start at your foundation. By identifying the risks and obstacles in your journey, we can prepare for the worst-case scenario. We can strategically and deliberately grow, resolving risks as we create rewards.

You might think that risk management is just something you do when your business is in trouble. But in fact, it's a skill that every small business owner should have.

Understanding risks is important because they help you plan for the future. When you know what could go wrong before it does, you can take steps to prevent it or prepare yourself for dealing with it when it does happen. Successful businesses aren't created by accident. With a solid defense, you can pave the path toward your goals and grow, despite any obstacles that lie in your path.

CHAPTER 2:

MAPPING OUT YOUR PATH TO GROWTH

Even when the unexpected strikes, risk management empowers us to take it with stride, supported by our defensive strategy against the inevitable change that comes with growth.

THE FIRST STEP TO GROWTH IS ESTABLISHING A BASELINE. Growth is increasing, strengthening, or improving from our present state. We can't track this growth if we don't establish a baseline control, or "Point A."

Point A

The first step toward sustainable growth is analyzing and understanding where you are now in your business. You might begin by asking yourself two basic questions:

- What's working well for my business?
- What's *not* working well for my business?

From here, we can use a basic SWOT Analysis to determine where your business currently lies in regard to the market. A SWOT Analysis guides you in examining your business's primary *Strengths, Weaknesses, Opportunities,* and *Threats.* Strengths and Weaknesses are *internal* factors affecting your business, such as your brand reputation, quality control, and the efficiency of your team. Opportunities and Threats are *external* factors affecting your business, such as market trends, competitors, and current events.

Point B

We'll examine these closer in our upcoming chapters. For now, we're simply mapping out the path to growth from Point A to Point B. But what *is* Point B for your business?

Imagine what "success" looks like for your company. When you picture growth, how does it look and feel? Can you quantify it? Perhaps you are able to hire a manager to give you more time to work *on* your business, rather than *in* it. Maybe it's franchising your store, opening a new product line, or hiring a team of professionals. Perhaps it's reaching a certain amount in sales, signing on a specific number of clients, or scaling the value and pricing of your offerings.

As a small business, it's important to have a clear idea of your growth goals. This will help you make informed decisions about how to allocate your resources and manage potential risks.

Point A + x = Point B

Now, for the final part of the equation. How do we solve the problem of getting from Point A to Point B? The solution is actually quite simple: Point A + x = Point B.

To solve for x, we must calculate the difference between where you *want* to be vs. where you *currently* are in your business. For example, suppose you want to hire a manager. In that case, you need to scout talent, create an effective onboarding and training system, and ensure you have the funds in place to pay them. If you want to increase sales, you need to increase your investment in marketing, brand positioning, and overall sales efforts.

Yet, it's easier said than done. There's inherent risk involved in expanding your team and passing on management outside ownership. If you're not careful, you can spend more on marketing efforts than what you get in return. In seeking any reward, we face risks. How can we identify which risks present more opportunities vs. threats? How can we decrease the threats and amplify the opportunities for growth?

Remember: We are hard-wired to manage risks. To understand this, we must examine risk psychology.

Your Relationship with Risk

Risks are the variable factors in our growth equation. If we don't factor them into our growth strategies, we'll under- or overestimate our plans and miscalculate the path to success. This is primarily because risk-taking is an emotional judgment. Using the SP/A Theory, we can understand why and how people respond to risks. The SP/A Theory (security-potential/aspiration) proposes that when faced with risks, we make decisions based on three emotions: the drive to reduce fear and provide security, finding hope and faith to resolve a problem, and the motivation or aspiration to reach our greatest goals. In short, risk-based decisions are built on three instinctual emotions: *fear, hope,* and *motivation.*

Fear is ingrained into our DNA. It's a tool used to allow us to flee and survive life-threatening situations. In our nervous systems, this mechanism is called "fight or flight," a natural response to fear and threats. If fear-driven business owners identify a risk, they are often urged to avoid it at all costs.

Some risks inspire business owners to discover hope. This is familiar for optimists and chronic risk-takers who only focus on the reward aspect of the risk-reward spectrum.

Finally, risks can often ignite our brains to take action, giving us the motivation to overcome, fight, and achieve success. We see a risk and view it as a challenge.

Each business owner and individual has a unique risk-management type. Some are more prone to fear, while others hope or drive. Understanding your personal biases, habits, and perceptions of risks will empower self-awareness in your business decisions. This is key, as our mere reactions to risk can be riskier than the threat itself. Recognize your relationship with risk — do you make judgments based on your senses, or do you rely on your intuition or "gut instinct?" Have you avoided risk in the past out of luck or deliberate planning? As a whole, humans tend to be overconfident in their ability to control risks. This is how we are able to intentionally go through with decisions that we fully understand pose a threat to our safety and security; yet, it's also why we make so many mistakes and, arguably, why 90% of startups fail.

Psychologists Daniel Kahneman and Amos Tversky developed the framework called "prospect theory." Prospect theory also questions why we take some risks yet avoid others. Many of us carefully select insurance plans to protect our health, yet we go skydiving, eat junk food, or refuse to visit the doctor; we buy car insurance and fasten our seatbelts, but we knowingly take illegal U-turns and drive past the speed limit; we quit our 9-5s to start our own businesses, yet we often find it difficult to invest any money into them. Kahneman and Tversky's prospect theory answers this question by understanding our perception of risk. This perception is greatly influenced by two cognitive patterns: *loss aversion* and *framing*. *Loss aversion* explains how most people experience loss more intensely than gains. For example, losing $100 is more painful than gaining $100 is rewarding. So, if a risk requires us to lose, invest, or miss out either initially or equally, we're not likely to take it. However, this isn't the only factor in play. Framing plays a significant role in our relationships with risk, as well as overall decisions and attitudes in life. Framing implies that we're more influenced by the context and phrasing of a risk than the risk itself. For example, if you were told you had a 50% chance of succeeding in your business, you might feel hope. But if I were to tell you there's a 50% chance your business will fail, you'll start to lose hope. Both statistics hold the same meaning: it's only how we frame it that we apply it. This reveals the immense power of our mindsets.

Growth Mindset vs. Fixed Mindset

Growing up in the concrete jungle, New York City, was a life experience that constantly challenged me. The city never sleeps has a unique, fast-paced atmosphere that can be both invigorating and overwhelming. As I navigated my way through life and work in NYC, I faced a multitude of difficulties and obstacles that shaped my perspective *and* resilience.

In the early stages of my career, I encountered several challenges that made me question my abilities and decisions. I struggled to make a name for myself in the highly competitive NYC market and found it difficult to balance work, life, and personal growth. It was during this time that I realized the importance of having an open mindset and the ability to adapt to change. New York City offers a wealth of opportunities, yet it can also become an insular environment that narrows one's perspective. In some respects, the city functions as a self-contained universe, which may inadvertently disconnect its inhabitants from the broader reality.

As a small business owner, I learned that risks are an integral part of growth and development. By taking the time to assess the risks I faced, I was able to develop a plan to minimize their impact on my business. Business growth is a combination of offensive and defensive strategies. As I worked to increase the rewards, I simultaneously honed my skills to dodge and fight against potential risks.

The turning point for me was when I decided to expand my business to the Netherlands. This decision was not made lightly, as I knew that it would involve a significant amount of risk and uncertainty. I was relocating to a country where English is not the primary language, and the cultural landscape differs greatly from that of NYC. However, I trusted my instincts and took the leap of faith, believing that my open mindset would guide me through the process.

Upon moving to the Netherlands, I felt liberated from the constraints of my previous life in NYC. The new environment allowed me to further cultivate my open mindset and tap into previously unexplored potential. I embraced the unique opportunities and challenges that the Netherlands had to offer, and my business flourished as a result.

The new environment helped me to reassess my priorities and find a renewed sense of purpose. The experiences I gained from living and working in NYC still inform my approach to business, but I have learned to adapt and evolve in the face of new challenges.

My journey from New York City to the Netherlands has been a transformative experience that has taught me invaluable lessons about risk management and personal growth. By embracing an open mindset and facing challenges head-on, I have been able to achieve success in both my personal and professional life. As a small business owner, it is essential to recognize that growth is a continuous process that requires the ability to adapt, learn, and overcome adversity. Our environment plays a crucial role in shaping our mindset, growth, and overall well-being. My new risk environment became a healthy place where I can foster personal and professional development by encouraging individuals to step out of their comfort zones and embrace new opportunities.

In a healthy risk environment, individuals are exposed to a variety of challenges and experiences that can help them build resilience and adaptability. This, in turn, allows them to develop a growth mindset, which is characterized by the belief that intelligence, talents, and abilities can be cultivated through hard work, dedication, and perseverance. Failure is viewed as a learning opportunity rather than a setback. This perspective fosters resilience and encourages individuals to take calculated risks in pursuit of their goals. Embracing the notion that failure is a natural part of growth can help mitigate the fear of failure and promote a positive mindset. My failures in New York City created opportunities for me.

As we see, even our mindset around risks affects our decision-making, confidence, and security. In growing your business, you must adopt a *growth mindset*. Coined by Dr. Carol Dweck, an individual with a growth mindset believes success is achieved, earned, and developed. It's a potential to be created, strategized, and worked toward. Those with a *fixed mindset* believe the opposite: that success skills are a product of luck and good genes.

A founder with a *growth* mindset will see their business as a blank canvas for them to paint their own masterpiece. By identifying potential risks, they understand they can take control of their business's outcome. But a founder with a *fixed* mindset views both risks and rewards as products of luck — factors outside of their control. Studies show those with a growth mindset achieve and accomplish much more than those with a fixed mindset. A growth mindset is essential for taking strategic risks, making profitable decisions, and reducing threats to help your business grow. With a fixed mindset, you're more likely to let inaction take the steering wheel, leaving your greatest weaknesses vulnerable to risks and threats.

Before you can grow, you must understand what factors are responsible for this growth potential. While we can't plan for and predict everything, we have immense control over our businesses and our lives. Even when the unexpected strikes, risk management empowers us to take it with stride, supported by our defensive strategy against the inevitable change that comes with growth.

As a small business owner, you face many risks on a daily basis. By taking the time to assess the risks you face, you can develop a plan to minimize their impact on your business. Business growth is an offensive and defensive strategy — as you increase the rewards, you must learn to dodge and fight against the risks.

Are you experiencing a fixed mindset and you wish to expand out, schedule a 30 mins call to see how we can work together to get you on the growth mindset, **https://calendly.com/rhysli-co/30min**

Part II: Getting to Know Your Enemy #1

CHAPTER 3:

IDENTIFYING THE RISKS & OBSTACLES IN YOUR JOURNEY

Every business's greatest weakness lies in rigidity and resistance to risks, rather than the risks themselves.

EVERY BUSINESS OWNER FACES RISKS, BUT NOT EVERY BUSINESS OWNER KNOWS HOW TO IDENTIFY AND MANAGE THEM EFFECTIVELY. Risk management is a critical part of any business growth strategy. Similarly, to how addressing life's risks can foster personal development, the same principle applies to nurturing growth within your business. Effectively handling risks can aid in identifying and mitigating potential threats to your business.

What is Risk Management?

Risk management is the process of identifying the potential risks that could impact your business and taking steps to minimize those risks or mitigate their impact. Risk management can be applied to any aspect of your business, from finances and operations to marketing and sales. As a result, it's important that you take a holistic approach when identifying and addressing risks. You should consider how each aspect of your business interacts with others and how each new decision could affect every other area of your organization. By taking a proactive approach to risk management, you can identify potential problems early and take steps to avoid them.

This is the foundation of risk management — solving problems by anticipating them. Whether this allows us to reduce the negative impact or avoid the threat as a whole, risk management is a catalyst to business growth.

Yet, risk management is not just an exercise in mapping out all of the bad things that could happen; it's also an opportunity to identify what will help mitigate those risks and turn them into opportunities. With a deliberate strategy, you can turn obstacles into springboards to climb toward your goals.

Types of Risks

Business risk is any exposure a company has that threatens its ability to function and succeed. Business risks can limit growth and even lead to failure. These risks can stem from external factors, internal traits, or often a combination of both. Most business risks can be categorized into four unique types: compliance risks, operational risks, reputational risks, and strategic risks.

Compliance risks are any threats your company faces due to industry regulations. For example, if you are a real estate agent, you must abide by federal and state real estate laws and regulations to maintain your license. If you're a restaurant owner, you must ensure you have the licenses needed to handle and sell food, as well as maintain compliance with cleanliness and quality standards. If you don't comply, you're at risk of losing your business.

Operational risks stem from your business's systems, workflows, and processes. If your processes are inefficient, you're at risk of losing profits and resources. These are often difficult to spot, as many owners have a blindspot to their own habits and procedures.

Reputational risks are any events that can damage the relationship between a brand and its customers. In today's social media world, many brands face reputational risks every time they post online. However, maintaining a strong online presence is essential for most businesses. As a result, owners and managers need a deliberate reputation protection plan to retain customer relations.

Strategic risks arise when a business strays from its strategy. For example, if a brand known for selling affordable goods tries selling luxury goods, they move away from its business model and strategy. While some strategic risks pay off, most make it difficult for businesses to reach their goals and unclear for customers to understand their brand positioning.

Identify Your Risks

The first step in risk management is to *identify* your risks. As a small business, you are likely to face many risks. Some of these risks may be due to your own weaknesses. For example, you may not have the financial resources, brand recognition, or system to scale your growth. Know what your company's risks are, and identify them early on. This will help you prevent any potential problems before they happen.

We'll begin by examining the *internal* landscape of your business to reinforce your foundation for growth. In our accompanying course, *How to Identify Risks in Your Business: A Small Business Owner's 5-Step Guide to Successful Growth,* we use a SWOT Analysis to map out these internal factors, beginning with our *Strengths*. For free SWOT Analysis template visit: **www.rhysli.co/SWOTanalysis**.

SWOT Analysis: *Strengths*

Strengths are your value proposition — the elements and attributes that set you apart from your competitors. Uncover your strengths by considering the following questions:

- What are my business's assets?
- What are my greatest selling points?
- What generates the most profits in my business?
- What is most efficient about my business?

Reflect on your financial assets, human resources, the quality of your product or service, and your operational systems as a whole. You can identify your strengths using data from financial reports, web analytics, customer reviews, and employee feedback.

SWOT Analysis: *Weaknesses*

These strengths can be compromised by your company's *Weaknesses*. Weaknesses create holes and cracks in your business's foundation, slowly chipping away at everything you've worked for. By identifying your weaknesses, you reinforce your strengths and advantages. These are internal factors putting your company at risk. Identify your weaknesses by considering the following questions:

- What are your liabilities?
- What are you most vulnerable to?
- Where are you losing the most money?
- Where are you losing the most time?

Like strengths, weaknesses can be found in your financial resources, human resources, the quality of your product or service, and your operational systems. You can identify these by analyzing your reports, business history, and feedback from customers and employees alike. By identifying your risks, you can begin to create a plan to mitigate them.

In our accompanying course, we identify the most common risks businesses faced in 2022. These were ranked as follows:

- Cyber Incidents: *44%*
- Business Interruption: *42%*
- Natural Catastrophes: *25%*

- Pandemic Outbreak: *22%*
- Legislation Changes: *19%*
- Climate Change: *17%*
- Market Changes: *15%*
- Skilled Employee Shortage: *13%*

Your business is likely threatened by many of these risks — but which are you *most* vulnerable to? This depends on your industry, competitors, market, human resources, operational systems, and financial standing.

As we can see, the most common risk faced by small businesses is the threat of cyberattacks. These attacks can have a number of devastating effects, including the loss of sensitive data, the destruction of critical systems, and even reputational damage. In order to protect your business from these threats, it is important to have a robust cyber security plan in place. This plan should include measures such as data encryption, password protection, and regular system updates.

But how can you measure your *vulnerability* to this threat? This is where we examine business weaknesses. For example, you may be vulnerable to cyberattacks if your business is primarily online or, perhaps, if you and your team don't have any cybersecurity training or knowledge.

Strengths and weaknesses are more complex than your advantages and disadvantages; they measure your vulnerability and security against your greatest threats.

How Airbnb Turned its Weaknesses Into Strengths

Simply relying too much on one product, platform, or market trend can pose a risk. Take Airbnb, for example. Before the COVID-19 pandemic, Airbnb was valued at $31 billion. By April 2020, its valuation dropped to $18 billion — just over half its value a few months prior. Airbnb's strengths and weaknesses are innately connected. They offer flexible travel and serve a customer base of both guests *and* hosts. But, as with every other hospitality service, the company began to tank and laid off about 25% of its employees once customers no longer had the flexibility and opportunity to travel.

Its inherent weakness was that its success relied on one factor: the ability to travel. As a data-driven company, Airbnb realized this and adapted quickly. Analyzing their strengths, weaknesses, opportunities, and threats, the organization capitalized on long-term stays and Airbnb "Experiences." Hosts were able to rent out their properties without worrying about excessive foot traction, while local and online tours, classes, and events were hosted on the platform. By the end of 2020, Airbnb's valuation skyrocketed to $86.5 billion, profiting $219.3 in Q3.

Airbnb turned its weaknesses into strengths. While projected to fail because of its travel-based business model, it expanded its offerings to fit market needs and focused its marketing on accommodating the trends. This wouldn't have been possible without their dedication to data, understanding of their SWOT, and an operational system that allowed them to pivot and reposition.

As we see, every business's greatest weakness lies in *rigidity* and *resistance* to risks, rather than the risks themselves. Some risks, like global pandemics, can't be predicted. Yet, we can have a plan in place in case the unprecedented becomes our reality. While we can't predict the future, we can prepare for it — and that's your greatest defense against the unknown.

How a Tech Company Prevented New Risks

As a risk consultant and coach, I've assisted several companies to mitigate risks. These risks came about through the natural progress in the growth of the business. Some had a lack of control but most company faced new risks as its business grew. When it comes to risk, it also doesn't necessarily mean risk that impacts company directly. We need to focus on a department or a small process within the company.

An example where a company faced a new risk as it grew is a company I had consulted, EMS. EMS is a tech company based in Amsterdam, the Netherlands. The company was growing its client based exponentially. To ensure stability in its growth, we performed a SWOT analysis to determine if there were new areas of concern that would hinder its growth. As a result of the analysis performed, we noted that a potential process that could slow down its business and the key point of its growth was compliance to the company's objectives and regulations. Without proper compliant processes, the company would probably hit a speed bump in the future. To prevent this, our second step was to go through all their compliance programs and processes. Identifying this would not have occurred if we didn't perform the analysis. Additionally, EMS would probably not have faced this new risk if they were not experiencing growth.

EMS is just one example of a company where we performed an analysis to identify new threats.

Want to start your SWOT analysis? Sign up for free, **www.rhysli.co/SWOTanalysis**.

CHAPTER 4:
PREPARING FOR THE WORST-CASE SCENARIO

We can't grow without changing — yet, all changes pose risks. From this, we learn that managing growth means managing risks.

WHAT'S THE WORST THAT COULD HAPPEN? This is the question every business owner must ask themselves. This is reflected in the strengths and weaknesses of your business. What factors do your strengths rely on? What threats do your weaknesses make you most vulnerable to?

Effective risk management is essential for small business growth and success. In 2020, many businesses discovered a global pandemic was their worst-case scenario. Often, the *fragility* of our greatest strength can become our greatest weakness. For example, freelance graphic designers rely on their ability to access the internet. This allows them to communicate with clients, use specific software, and harness their unique skills to serve their clients around the world. But what if they lose access to the communication and creation platforms needed for their work? What if their data gets compromised and they lose their assets?

What if something happens to them and their ability to design — who will temporarily replace them?

Here, we shift to the *external* factors affecting our businesses. In the SWOT Analysis, these factors are your *Opportunities* and *Threats*.

SWOT Analysis: *Opportunities*

Opportunities are the potential decisions you can make to increase your success in the market. Opportunities can present themselves in the form of new trends, target audience expansion, technological innovations, and more. Harnessing our growth mindsets, we can carve out these opportunities for ourselves. By gathering market data, we can identify current trends in consumer behavior, demographics, and innovations and connect them with our strengths. This is what we call *leverage*. It's utilizing our internal strengths to take advantage of an external factor, creating a window of opportunity for growth.

Yet, when our weaknesses relate to our opportunities, we inhibit our ability to grow. This provides a headstart for competitors and dilutes our strengths. As we see, by identifying and patching up our weaknesses, we automatically increase our strengths, helping us grow.

SWOT Analysis: *Threats*

Like opportunities, *threats* are external factors that can affect business growth. Threats are the inherent risks our businesses face. This is your "worst-case scenario." Perhaps a natural disaster could destroy your inventory and disrupt your operations. You could be sued for damages if a customer is injured on your premises.

One of your key employees could leave, taking clients and knowledge with them. You could be the victim of a cyber attack, resulting in the loss of data and revenue. The list goes on.

These are just some of the risks that small businesses face, but they don't have to be paralyzing. For example, the right insurance plan can protect your business from natural disasters. Investment and training in safety standards can protect your employees from injury. A professional, thorough contract can keep your employees from leaving and taking your clients with them. Investing in cybersecurity and software can protect your data. As we see, solutions can be found once we identify and analyze these problems.

Pinpoint your threats by examining your business from an outside perspective:
- Where does my business stand against the competition?
- What potential policies and regulations might limit my business?
- What market, industry, or social change would cause me to lose my customers or clients?

When a threat affects your company's strengths, it increases your vulnerability. It weakens your strengths and puts you in a more vulnerable position to risks. When a weakness directly interacts with a threat, it becomes problematic. This is where the potential for failure becomes highly likely. For example, your business's greatest weakness may be a dependency on your small team of 3. You don't have the budget to hire more employees, which amplifies this weakness. If your greatest threats are the increasingly competitive nature of the industry and a harsh labor shortage, you are at an even *greater* risk of failure.

As we learned in our last chapter, one of the greatest weaknesses a business can have is rigidity and resistance toward adaptation. By identifying our opportunities and threats, we realize that our biggest threat is our resistance and response to *change*. The inability to adapt to change is the greatest risk your business faces. Isolate what changes you're most vulnerable to, and you'll identify your *Enemy #1*. Ironically, growth is all about change. We can't grow without changing — yet, all changes pose risks. From this, we learn that managing *growth* means managing *risks*.

As business owners with a growth mindset, we know this ability to adapt to change can be developed. Thus, our greatest defense against risks is to plan, prepare, and strengthen our abilities to adapt and respond to change.

These plans begin with us identifying our weaknesses and taking stock of what's at stake — your reputation, employees' livelihoods, and the money, time, and passion you've invested in growing your company. Know what's at stake to protect what's at stake.

CHAPTER 5:

GETTING TO KNOW YOUR RISK STAKEHOLDERS

*Change inspires growth and risk. The more
stakeholders involved, the more opportunity
and diversity your business has access to; and as
a result, the more risk stakeholders can affect or
be affected by your business's threats.*

AS A SMALL BUSINESS OWNER, YOU PLAY MANY ROLES:
You might be the CEO, the CFO, and the head of HR. As
the founder, you're also the primary leader for risk management. While this may seem like a daunting task, it's
essential to the sustainable growth of your business. By
understanding your risks and addressing them head-on,
you can create a plan for success.

This leads us to Step 2 of the risk management process:
Analyzing the risks. Once you've identified your worst-case
scenarios, you must analyze the scope, correlations, and
severity of the risks.

Formal risk management plans for businesses often use
a document outlining the purpose, background, scope,
policy, and approach to effectively prevent or respond

to potential risks. The scope statement is an agreement amongst the project team and stakeholders, relaying that each member understands the risks, their severity, their roles in risk management, and how they're expected to respond to them. As we begin to analyze our risks, we must outline the scope by identifying our *risk stakeholders*.

Analyzing Your Risk Stakeholders

Risk stakeholders are any individuals who may affect or be affected by your business's risks. These are any managers, employees, investors, partners, and even customers who are at risk due to your company's threats and weaknesses. For example, let's say you rely on a specific manufacturer to create your product. If that chain of custody gets interrupted or there's a problem with the product, anyone with financial investment or dependence on your company gets affected: this includes you, your partners, investors, employees, and customers. Yet, each member is affected in a different way. However, the extent to which this risk affects your stakeholders can tie back to the manufacturer, the manager in charge of communicating these updates, and the employees' response. As always, the owner or manager holds great responsibility for how this crisis is managed. With a proper plan in place for this incident, the company might not be affected badly; but *without* a proper plan, this can completely turn the company upside down. This applies to any type of risk: for example, if managers aren't strict on safety policies, it can lead to workplace accidents. Employees who aren't well-versed in cybersecurity can accidentally put your data at risk. Again, this all begins with the leader's communication and efforts to train, prepare, and guide their team.

Owners & Managers

Business owners and managers have the most at stake with every business risk. Even the way the management is structured can affect this outcome. Solopreneurs may enjoy the freedom and independence of going it alone, but they hold *all* responsibility and stake in their risks. They are unable to hand off tasks, collaborate, and get the support they need to grow. If a solo founder is sick or unable to complete a task, all other tasks and assets are affected.

Co-founders and joint-owned businesses escape some of these risks yet face new ones. Often, co-founders are family members or friends. Family-owned businesses add a layer of complexity to risks. While the homogeneity and likeness of a family can reduce some disagreements, running a business while maintaining intimate relationships can cause others. Studies show that family-owned and tight-knit co-founded businesses foster trust and a familiar, well-communicated structure. Yet, the comfort and ease of these relationships can lead to crossed boundaries and a lack of diverse strengths and talents. Non-familial companies can offer the reverse. They often lead to more conflict, less trust, more strategic success, out-of-the-box thinking, and effective problem-solving.

One study analyzed a family-owned nursery in Munich, Germany: a fourth-generation business that cultivates and sells flowers and plants. The business is managed by the corporate family, consisting of three family members. After examination, the study found that their greatest risks were a lack of skilled workers and unclear boundaries of succession – each a correlation to their management structure.

Analyzing the structure of ownership allows you to better understand the risks at stake and their severity, likelihood, and correlations. As a result, you can respond to these risks by creating a plan to defend your vulnerabilities and amplify your advantages.

Team Members

Team members are pivotal to a business's growth. Most businesses cannot scale their offerings without scaling their manpower. Owners and managers directly influence who's on the team — and team members can make or break the success of this growth. As you change the structure of your company, you increase the stakes, including how many risk stakeholders there are and the scope of the potential risks.

Adding team members adds responsibility and liability to the owner, particularly depending on the hiring structure. At first, many small businesses hire contract workers to reduce liability as they begin to scale and grow. But since there's less at stake for contractors, many may invest less into your company compared to an in-house employee. Yet, hiring an in-house employee too soon — or the *wrong* employee — can lead to much more serious damages, as you're now responsible for providing a stable job for both you and your employee.

Investors & Partners

To scale a business, you need to scale your capital. Many founders are primarily interested in building a great business rather than maximizing their profit or control over the venture. In this growth stage, many owners turn to investors to support their great ideas. While this can immensely pay off, it invites a whole world of change to your business. As we know, change inspires growth *and* risk. The more stakeholders involved, the more opportunity and diversity your business has access to; and as a result, the more risk stakeholders can affect or be affected by your business's threats.

As we all know, risk management is essential to maintaining a healthy business. The role that team members and hiring structures play in risk management can be complex, but it's also very crucial. Everyone has their own unique stake in the game, and each stakeholder will have different needs. Some stakeholders may want to be kept informed about risks; others might feel as though they don't need to be bothered with such things until they become actual issues.

Leaders within the company need to understand who these stakeholders are and their roles — and then make sure that the right people are getting the right information at the right time, so everyone stays on track with their respective goals. If business growth is a game, the risk is your greatest opponent. Structure your team and lead your business to success with a comprehensive strategy.

If you're unsure who the risk stakeholders are in your company or you need help identifying risk stakeholders, please visit **www.rhysli.co/riskstakeholderstemplate** for FREE templates.

Part III: Strategic Growth Strategies

CHAPTER 6:
OVERCOMING OBSTACLES BY EVALUATING RISKS

The key to risk management is knowing which risks are most threatening to your company so you can prioritize and allocate your time, money, and energy accordingly.

THERE'S NO DOUBT ABOUT IT: OBSTACLES ARE A PART OF LIFE. In fact, they're a big part of business. It's how you handle them that matters. When you have a plan in place to deal with risks, you'll be able to get through them more easily and come out stronger on the other side. The key is learning how to use risk management strategies effectively, which leads us to Step 3: *Evaluating the risks.*

In entrepreneurship, there will always be a risk to manage and a fire to put out. The key to risk management is knowing which risks are most threatening to your company so you can prioritize and allocate your time, money, and energy accordingly. To achieve this, you must learn how to evaluate risks using both qualitative and quantitative methods to minimize your company's exposure to risk.

Qualitative Risk Analysis

The key difference between qualitative and quantitative risk analyses is the values we use to rank each risk. Qualitative risks rate threats based on our *personal perception* of how likely and how severe a risk is to damage the company. Qualitative risk analyses should be used whenever there's a change. For example, when you start a new project, add a new product, restructure your teams, or simply perceive a new threat or weakness within your company. A qualitative approach allows you to factor in human and cultural factors your data might not take into account, which makes it an integral part of your decision-making and evaluation. Qualitative risk analyses can be conducted as follows:

1. *Identify the risk.*
2. *Rank the risk based on probability and impact (see Chapter 10).*
3. *Pinpoint the root cause of the risk.*
4. *Resolve and control the risk.*
5. *Evaluate and monitor the results.*

Quantitative Risk Analysis

Quantitative risk analyses use data to calculate and estimate the outcome and likelihood of the threat. These should be conducted when the risk is heavily data-driven, such as financial decisions, brand positioning, and competitive strategies. When a manager isn't able to create a confident judgment based on perception, they must turn to data to ensure strategic results. A quantitative approach empowers systematic, strategic structures you can rely on. Every risk analysis should be evaluated based on the best, most accurate, up-to-date information available. Quantitative risk analyses are conducted as follows:

1. *Identify the goal and method of the risk analysis.*
2. *Establish the data and resources needed.*
3. *Conduct the analysis.*
4. *Evaluate the results.*
5. *Create and implement strategic control.*

By combining each type of analysis, we create a complete 'left brain and right brain' strategy, using facts and intuition to predict the future. Qualitative methods involve analyzing information from your gut feelings and intuition — you might ask yourself questions like: *"What would happen if x happened?" "Will this be an ongoing problem?"* or *"How could I solve this?"* Quantitative methods involve gathering data on similar situations, past performance, and analytics reports to make predictions based on data points.

Combining each of these methods, we're left with a ranking of how probable the risk is and its potential impact. These scores combine to calculate the risk level — which reveals how we should prioritize our efforts. But before we can reach this estimate, we must fully understand how to conduct these analyses and research. Data is power, but you can't access its strength unless you know how to find it.

CHAPTER 7:

INTERNAL RESEARCH: STRATEGIC GROWTH

*By knowing the root cause of our risk, we can
pull out the weeds, lay a solid foundation, and
transform weaknesses into strengths.*

TO IDENTIFY THE ROOT CAUSE OF A RISK, BUSINESS
OWNERS NEED TWO PERSPECTIVES: *Internal* and
External. Internal research requires business owners
and stakeholders to detect, evaluate, and control the
risk based on their in-house data and perspectives. We'll
begin here. As you identify your business's risks, we must
solve them at the root, not just on the surface.

For example, let's say your company's greatest risk is a
market change. However, this is the surface-level risk —
the *cause* lies in your company's weaknesses and threat
analyses. Risks are often caused by natural, human, or
economic events. From a fixed mindset, we can view
"market changes" as an ominous, unpredictable force
that could strike at any time, leaving our businesses
defenseless. But from a growth mindset, we can view
market changes as a natural, expected evolution of

the market. By understanding how much we rely on a market trend, we can identify our strengths, weaknesses, opportunities, and threats. From this perspective, we see that relying on one sector or creating trend-based offerings is the root cause of the risk. In response, we can set up a system and plan to diversify our income or adapt to new market trends. By knowing the root cause of our risk, we can pull out the weeds, lay a solid foundation, and transform weaknesses into strengths. Let's reveal the power of internal research for risk management and business growth by looking at real-world examples.

Case Study: The Power of Adapting & Data

Coffman Engineers is one of the top engineering firms in the world. In the past, they used standard phone services to communicate with their employees. But after one of their branches experienced a communication disaster, they pivoted and implemented cloud-based phone plans for all of their employees to prevent the issue from happening again. Based on the quantitative analysis, a cloud-based phone service would cost the company 50% more per employee compared to its previous phone plan. However, after further analyzing their internal research from the incident, they estimated the investment would actually save them money (25% per employee) thanks to damage prevention and additional communication features.

Risk management is the process of identifying and evaluating potential threats to your business so that you can make smart decisions about where and how to allocate resources. Coffman Engineers learned from the past to prepare for the future. By analyzing the costs of past threats, they could create a strategic plan that prevented damages while also saving money and streamlining processes.

Case Study: The Power of Strategic Growth

As of Q2 in 2022, Spotify had 188 million premium subscribers. Just five years prior, they had *half* the amount of paying customers. Founded in 2006, the multi-billion-dollar music streaming platform was strategic about its growth strategy. Five years before launching in the U.S, Spotify tested its business model, beta launching in several European countries. As they tested their service, they were able to use their customer data and buyer personas to refine their brand positioning and revamp their business strategy. This systematic launch not only gave them the data they needed to improve their business, but it provided them with evidence and numbers to draw the attention of investors and partners: namely, *Facebook*. After just four months of its U.S. launch in 2011, Spotify's growth skyrocketed, attracting over 1 million visitors each month.

Spotify heavily relied on its internal research to implement its growth strategy. By gradually launching their services and testing the responses, they were able to mitigate risks and refine their product so that when they invested in a major launch, they'd be set up for success.

Case Study: The Power of Focused Growth

Uber took a similar approach during their company's growth stage. Valued at 56.84 billion in Q3, Uber once had small beginnings. In 2009, they sought to disrupt the cab industry, providing a new type of transportation method, specifically to the San Francisco area. This location was strategically chosen, as its taxi industry is hated and new technology loved by locals. Uber's growth has always been implemented city by city. With every location presenting unique threats and opportunities, this allowed Uber to establish their presence and grow quickly yet carefully.

Throughout this process, Uber continues to test and retest their services to consistently grow and manage risks. In 2018, Uber revealed it has over 1,000 test experiments running on its platform all the time. Whether testing new UX design or responses from unique demographics, Uber continually tests ways to grow, modify, and improve its products. This commitment to data collection and analysis provides them with the tools they need to resolve problems and take advantage of opportunities ahead of time.

Methods for Conducting Internal Research

As we see, data collection and internal research allow companies to predict the future — the overall goal of risk management and growth strategies. This information allows companies, even in their early days, to pinpoint the root causes of their threats and opportunities. In mapping out the root causes, business owners must *identify* potential risks, *detect* signs of oncoming risks, *analyze* risk stakeholders, *evaluate* the probability and impact of the risks, and *implement* controls and testing to ensure effectiveness.

To accomplish this, owners and managers need data. Internal research can come from a variety of sources, such as:

- Customer feedback and reviews
- Employee feedback
- Monthly, quarterly, and annual financial reports
- Safety reports
- A/B testing of marketing and communication strategies
- Competitor research
- Industry updates
- Market reports and trends
- Online and social media activity of your target audience

Organize a system to continually yet efficiently collect data using these strategies. Based on this information, you can establish and perform Standard Operating Procedures, Quality Assurance Systems, and Audits. Your Standard Operating Procedures should outline your daily workflows and processes as a company. This will clearly outline roles, expectations, and standards to ensure quality results and straightforward communication. By factoring in risk assessments and internal research into your Standard Operating Procedures, you can significantly avoid risk and direct your company toward sustainable growth.

Quality Assurance Systems ensure the same — by monitoring and collecting data concerning your company's output, you can better control it. Regular audits and inventory of your procedures and systems help you and your business to stay focused and efficient and, most importantly, be aware of any potential risks, weaknesses, and threats that can naturally arise. These systems also allow you to efficiently collect data around your processes, giving you the tools you need to respond to, repair, and resolve any risks.

Growing your company is an inside job — but spotting oncoming threats requires an outside observer. Every team needs a lookout, watchman, and guide to warn them of what lies ahead.

CHAPTER 8:

EXTERNAL RESEARCH: THE HERO'S GUIDE

By asking, "What's the worst that could happen?" we can pave the path to answer, "What's the best that could happen?"

EVERY HERO NEEDS A GUIDE. Every brave hero and mighty warrior has a mentor. A hero's origin story truly begins once they stumble across their teacher, coach, and guide, ready to share the map to the hero's destination.

Small business owners are heroes. You have a dream and a destination you're seeking. You have the strength, determination, and vision to make it happen. And to embark on this path toward growth, you need a guide to share this blueprint with you — someone who's helped many other heroes find their way from Point A to Point B before.

As a small business owner, you're proud of what you've built. In a way, your business is an extension of you. From a competitive lens, this gives you the unique advantage you need to rise above the ranks. But from a risk perspective, it can also give you a bias and blindspot of what lies ahead. While we're our worst critics, we're also our worst editors. As humans, it's inherently difficult to identify our own mistakes and weaknesses before it's too late. If you want to see your business grow and thrive, it's time for a reality check: Your business is not perfect. There are risks involved in every decision, every day. If you don't manage those risks effectively, they could sink your boat before it even leaves the harbor. One survey showed that 92% of CEOs viewed risk management as essential to long-term success and sustainable growth. Yet, only 23% of the same CEOS felt they had the data and resources to manage their risks.

Controlling the Risk with External Research

This leads us to Step 4 of the risk management process: *Controlling the risk*. External research is essential for not only identifying by resolving the root causes of your company's risk. External research takes the form of any third-party or outside observer with the expertise and experience to help assess, manage, and resolve your company's risks. Most often, external research is provided by risk management consultants and coaches who dedicate their careers to identifying and measuring risks and creating a strategy to integrate risk protection. As a result, this lays a solid foundation for business owners to grow, profit, and build their businesses with futuristic confidence.

As a risk management consultant of over 20 years, I've helped countless business owners identify risks *before* they become problems. I've analyzed these risks and evaluated them to determine which poses the greatest threat. And of course, I've created customized, deliberate strategies to learn from these threats and avoid them in the future. By combining internal research with external research, you capture every angle and brighten every blind spot in your risk management plan.

Case Study: A New Perspective for Profits

Sometimes problems just need a fresh set of eyes to find a solution. This was the real-world case of a small, local cleaning company we'll call "Cleaning Crew" for this story. The Cleaning Crew served both residential and commercial clients but spent most of their time serving residential clients. They knew they were threatened by their low-profit margins, inefficiency, and inconsistent clientele — but they weren't able to identify the root cause or, more importantly, a solution to move forward. After hiring a consultant, they were able to recognize the excessive amount of time, money, and resources consumed by their residential services. At the same time, commercial client projects were much more profitable. By analyzing their clientele, price structure, and costs, the consultant was able to create a new strategy that allocated resources to profitable efforts and mitigated risks by pulling away from profit-draining efforts. To ensure threats were low and opportunities were high, they guided the Cleaning Crew to create Standard Operating Procedures and Quality Assurance Systems to ensure clear communication and consistent results. Six months after implementing this strategy, Cleaning Crew experienced an increase in client retention — and a 56% increase in net profits.

Success lies in the structure of your organization. Inefficiencies cost, even if you don't recognize it. By identifying the risks, weaknesses, and threats of Cleaning Crew with external research, we can see how deliberate communication, strategies, and systems can mitigate risks and create opportunities for growth.

Risk Management Consultants: The Hero's Guide

This is just one example of the power of leveraging external research to resolve risks at their roots. Yet, for this process to work, businesses need to partner with the right consultant. Risk management consultants are professionals trained to help organizations identify, analyze, and minimize risk and loss. This includes detecting risks, measuring their severity and probability, creating a plan, and most importantly, helping implement it. As we learn, establishing effective systems can proactively solve and prevent problems before they occur. The best part? Risk management consultants can do all of this from the outside looking in — which means they'll give you unbiased advice that's not subdued by any personal feelings or bias.

Risk management is all about preparing for the future — but it shouldn't turn into fearing the future. When owners and founders conduct risk management alone, they're left calculating and stressing over numbers and elements they can't control. When guided by a professional, risk management turns away from fearing the future and shifts toward welcoming it. We fear the future because of the unknowns. The "what-ifs." But when you're prepared, these unknowns become opportunities, possibilities, and tokens of freedom. The "what-ifs" represent your potential growth and limitless capacities. Your potential should never be held back by unnecessary risks.

By asking, "What's the *worst* that could happen?" we can pave the path to answer, "What's the *best* that could happen?"

If you feel trapped or would want to know more how risk coaching/consulting can help, schedule a FREE meeting with me at **https://calendly.com/rhysli-co/30min**

CHAPTER 9:
BEST PRACTICES IN RISK MANAGEMENT

As you face risk head-on,
you can clear the path to growth.

SMALL BUSINESS OWNERS CAN'T AFFORD TO TAKE BIG RISKS. You've got too much on the line to gamble with your cash flow, and you've got too many people relying on your success. Yet, you know that taking risks is what it means to be an entrepreneur. You have to be willing to bet on yourself in order for your business to grow. So how do you find that balance? By evaluating risks using both qualitative and quantitative methods — and then coming up with practical strategies for dealing with each one of them.

As we've learned to identify, analyze, and evaluate risks, we must take our internal and external research to *control* and *resolve* the risk. Risk management isn't just about identifying potential problems; it's also about taking action when those problems arise. Once you identify a risk, there are four strategies you can take to reduce its impact on your company:

The 4 Risk Management Strategies

Avoidance: You may be able to avoid the risk altogether by not doing something that could cause trouble later on down the line. For example, a construction company might be at risk of workplace accidents, particularly slips and falls. They might choose to build low-rise buildings to avoid extreme heights. Or, a business might handle highly sensitive information from its clients. They might limit the number of employees who can access this data to prevent it from being compromised.

While not all risks can be eliminated, risk avoidance strategies can reduce the number of weaknesses and vulnerabilities a business has to manage.

Transfer: Another approach you can take is the risk transfer strategy. If one stakeholder is responsible for a large portion of the risk, you can transfer this risk to share with others. A common risk transfer strategy is purchasing insurance for your business. If there's a natural disaster or workplace incident, the right insurance policy can transfer some of the loss and mitigation from your business to the insurance provider. Understand what insurance policies will cover in case of an accident or other unforeseen event.

Reduction: When evaluating risks, we must estimate their probability and impact. Rather than aiming to avoid the risk altogether, reduction strategies aim to reduce the level of probability and impact. For example, the construction company at risk of slips and falls can provide quality equipment and safety gear, safety checklists, regular site safety audits, and ongoing OSHA training to reduce the likelihood and severity of the risks.

Acceptance: Evaluating risks gives us the perspective needed to properly prioritize risk management efforts. Suppose a risk has a low probability and low impact score. In that case, we may take an acceptance strategy — A.K.A., don't take any action against it. This is only effective when resources are needed to resolve other risks or the cost of managing the risk is equal to or greater than the estimated cost of the risk itself.

Top-Down Approach

One of the most important roles of an owner and manager is to protect the company from oncoming threats. While there are many different ways to approach risk management, the top-down approach proves itself time and time again. Risk management starts with management teams. Whether you have one partner or 20 employees, risk culture begins at the top. When assessing risks, involve every risk stakeholder. Agree on each member's responsibilities and roles in avoidance, reduction, transfer, and acceptance. Leaders should be tasked to organize, inform, and implement these plans across the company through clear, consistent systems, such as the Standard Operating Procedures and Quality Assurance Systems. If owners don't abide by these themselves, neither will their employees. Create set plans and communicate these expectations to every risk stakeholder. By taking full accountability for your risk management, you can maintain control. Of course, this doesn't mean leading and managing risks solo. Every member should play a crucial role in avoiding and mitigating risks, and risk consultants can help assign and organize these systems.

Proactivity Over Reactivity

Most business owners wait for problems to present themselves — but you're not most business owners. The key to sustainable growth is to be proactive rather than reactive. Proactivity is thinking ahead and planning for the future, whether opportunities or threats. Instead of cleaning up messes, it tasks us to continually tidy up and keep watch on our business processes. This approach requires us to continually monitor, audit, and communicate our workflows and standards. For example, you can take a proactive approach to avoid reputational risks by continually monitoring your online social channels and staying up-to-date on social and cultural expectations. You can even prevent cybersecurity threats by continually monitoring your systems and training employees on the latest hacking, scamming, and phishing attacks. Be one step ahead of your threats, and you'll find more room for growth.

Maintain Balance & Keep Moving

Some risks require avoidance, while others may call for an acceptance strategy. In finding and maintaining balance, ensure to clearly address the potential consequences you and your team face. Avoiding risk doesn't mean avoiding talking about risk — in fact, it's the opposite. Face uncertainty and address the potential of loss. As you face risk head-on, you can clear the path to growth. It's in overcoming and rising above our threats and weaknesses that we find strength and create opportunities.

Even with the most strategic of plans, life is full of surprises. As you identify and face new risks, make room for change. Remember: If rigidity to change is our greatest weakness, flexibility is our greatest strength. Be open to adapting, and you'll reframe risks as mere bumps in the road on your journey toward growth.

CHAPTER 10:
BUILDING YOUR RISK MANAGEMENT TOOLBELT

As we prepare for the worst, we can rise above it.

SO MANY SMALL BUSINESSES FAIL BECAUSE THEY DON'T DO THEIR HOMEWORK. A solid risk management toolbelt will help you prepare for any scenario — and even better, it'll help keep your business safe and growing in the long term. Risk management isn't about crossing your fingers and hoping for the best. It's about using a wide range of tools to ensure that your business is protected from the dangers that lurk in every corner. It's not enough to just try to make money. You need to understand and control the risks in your business, but you don't have to do it alone. In fact, the more tools and resources you use, the more efficient and accurate your efforts can be. As a risk consultant, I'm going to share three tools I use to protect and prepare clients for the *worst-case* scenario so they can empower the *best-case* scenario:

Risk Heat Map

A risk heat map is a color-coded tool that helps you visualize all of your risks in order of their likelihood and impact, so you can understand where your biggest vulnerabilities are. On one axis, the map will categorize the probability of a risk event; on the other, it will rank its potential severity of impact. By automatically combining and comparing the probability and impact of each risk, you can easily interpret which threats you're most vulnerable to. From here, you can take action and prioritize each risk in order of importance. Risks with the highest score will require your greatest attention and resources to avoid, prevent, and transfer any damage. Risks with low scores may permit an acceptance strategy. Risks with high probability yet low impact scores need close monitoring yet few allocated resources; risks with high impact scores yet low probability scores may require a transfer strategy to lessen liability.

Is a risk heat map genuinely beneficial for a small business? Absolutely! I was approached by a small bakery in Amsterdam to assist them in identifying areas that the owner and baker may have overlooked. By applying a risk heat map, we were able to pinpoint critical risks, develop effective mitigation strategies, and prevent potential disruptions that could have resulted in financial losses or even business failure. This proactive approach to risk management ensured the ongoing stability and success of their bakery.

The first approach we performed was listing potential risks that impact or could impact the business. We identified risks such as fluctuations in ingredient prices, equipment breakdown, employee turnover, and changes in consumer preferences. Thereafter, we assessed the likelihood and impact of each risk, concluding that equipment breakdown and fluctuations in ingredient prices were the most critical threats. After careful analysis, the baker was then able to plot the risks on the heat map, revealing that equipment breakdown and fluctuations in ingredient prices fell into the high-priority (red zone) category. We then developed strategies to address the high-priority risks. For equipment breakdown, they invested in preventive maintenance and established a relationship with a reliable repair service. To manage ingredient price fluctuations, they diversified their suppliers and negotiated long-term contracts to secure more stable prices. By applying a risk heat map to their small business, the baker was able to identify and prioritize critical risks, develop effective mitigation strategies, and avoid potential disruptions that could have led to financial losses or even business failure. This proactive approach to risk management ensured the ongoing stability and success of her business.

Book time with me if you need information on how to set up your first Risk Heat Map (make sure you mention Risk Heat Map in your message) **https://calendly.com/rhysli-co/30min**

Root Cause Analysis

Business owners can learn one of the greatest lessons from the legend of the Hydra. In Greek mythology, the hero Hercules was tasked to slay the seven-headed monster. According to the myth, as soon as any hero cut one head off, two would grow back in place of it. It was only thanks to the help of Hercules' guide that he found the root cause of this problem and defeated the monster.

Too often, we try to solve the surface-level problem, only to find two "heads" or risks beneath it. Root cause analyses act as our guides to trace back to the center of the problem. A root cause analysis is a strategic examination of what's causing problems within your business. You can find solutions that fix those root causes, rather than Band-Aid solutions. This strategy allows you to look at your business from different angles, specifically:

- *What? (Problem)*
- *How? (Causes)*
- *Why? (Root Causes)*

The most important part is asking why *multiple* times. Be curious — this helps you figure out *what* happened, *how* it happened, and *why* it was able to happen so you can identify where things went wrong and how to improve them. For example, let's say your team suffered a phishing attack. While it's easy to pin this on one person or factor, most risks are multi-layered.

What? — One of your team members accidentally sent over sensitive data to a cybercriminal pretending to be a manager.

How? — The phishing scam looked legitimate, and the employee wasn't aware of the signs of these types of attacks.

Why? — The employee wasn't provided the necessary training to identify these types of attacks; there wasn't a company policy about what information can and can't be shared via email; there wasn't a regulation in place to control what data employees have access to; managers were also unaware of these types of phishing scams and how to identify them.

As you continually ask why a problem occurred, you can get to the root cause and resolve it to prevent similar issues from happening in the future.

Business Continuity Plan

Growth starts at the foundation, just as risk management starts with systems. 3 in 4 businesses have no emergency preparedness plans in place. This is especially vital for threats like cyberattacks. Research shows that 96% of companies with a disaster response plan were able to survive cyberattacks, but 93% of companies *without* a plan had to shut down their business within 12 months.

A Business Continuity Plan (BCP) is a powerful system you can use to prepare and plan ahead. BCPs outline exactly what your business will do in case something goes wrong, whether a fire, flood, pandemic, or cyberattack. The goal of a BCP is to reduce any interruption in service or productivity during an emergency situation.

It should outline:
- *Potential risks*
- *How these risks may impact operations*
- *What actions need to be taken to mitigate these risks, including who needs to be notified, necessary procedures, who is responsible for each task, and how long each task will take.*
- *Key objectives of the overall continuity plan.*

The risks included in your BCP should be the risks with the highest probability and impact. However, creating a BCP isn't a one-time task. You should test the plan to see if it will work and continually review and update the plan to include any new risks or factors.

Variance and Trend Analysis

While strategies and plans are essential for growth, we can't forget to look at the facts. Variance and trend analysis is the practice of looking at the difference between your *expected* results and the *actual* results. From here, you can better figure out what's causing that difference. It helps you identify areas where you can improve, control your business growth, and make better decisions. As you identify any deviations from the norm, you can spot early warning signs of any risks lying ahead.

Variance analysis involves comparing actual results against planned and/or historical data. Suppose you're running a retail store, for example. In that case, you might want to compare this month's sales figures with the same period last year so you can see any trends emerging over time (such as an overall increase or decrease). Trend analysis is similar in concept, but instead of looking at differences between actual and expected numbers, it looks for changes in those numbers over time. Suppose you have a consistent trend of low sales volume. In that case, this is an excellent indicator that something needs to change — either with your marketing strategy or with the product itself.

By looking to the past, we can prepare for the future. We must learn from our mistakes today and yesterday to avoid future risks. This is the common thread in each of our risk strategy tools. As we prioritize our threats, we can use our energy and resources wisely. As we challenge ourselves to ask why a problem happened, we can get to the root of it. As we prepare for the worst, we can rise above it. As we check in on our goals, we can redirect our sails and journey forward toward growth.

Part IV: Deliberate Results

CHAPTER 11:

GROWING FORWARD

As we look forward, we grow forward.

MANAGING RISKS ISN'T A ONE-TIME EVENT, JUST LIKE GROWTH ISN'T ACHIEVED OVERNIGHT. We know that Step 1 of risk management begins with *identifying* risks. Step 2 *analyzes* risks, Step 3 *evaluates* risks, and Step 4 *controls* the risk. Lastly, Step 5 *monitors* the risk.

Step 5: Monitoring Risks

Business owners must be diligent, keeping a close eye on the risk mitigation process and its effectiveness. This is where we learn the most: the value of our risk data, strategy, and efforts. When monitoring a risk, we must assess how well the response policies and procedures were followed and if our plans were accurate. Steps 1-4 are all prediction-based. We make educated assumptions about our "what-ifs" and plan, act, and respond accordingly. In monitoring, we can test how correct and effective these predictions were. If there are any holes or errors, we can fill in the gaps, modifying our risk management tools and data to reinforce our defenses for the future.

As a business owner, you're probably thinking you don't have time to monitor risks. The only think you want to monitor is your business operations. Yes, rightfully so but monitoring your risks is also monitoring your operations. When the owners of a café shop hired me to help them with their business, they were reluctant at first to apply this step. Their response was that they are a small shop, and they need to concentrate on the operations of the café. During our initial meeting, I asked for their back story of the café shop. After our conversation, the owners recognized the importance of risk management and took steps to identify and address potential threats to their business. They began by identifying a range of risks, such as changes in consumer preferences, supply chain disruptions, fluctuations in coffee bean prices, and competition from larger coffee chains. We worked together to address these concerns. We created several proactive measures to mitigate any of the risks they mentioned. These were the approach we took:

1. Diversifying their coffee bean suppliers to ensure a steady supply and minimize the impact of price fluctuations or supply chain disruptions.

2. Staying informed of industry trends and customer preferences, which allowed them to adapt their menu and offerings to cater to evolving tastes and dietary requirements.

3. Developing a strong brand identity that emphasized the quality of their coffee, their commitment to sustainability, and their support for local artists. This helped differentiate them from larger coffee chains and attracted a loyal customer base.

4. Implementing rigorous food safety and hygiene practices to reduce the risk of health violations and maintain a positive reputation.
5. Regularly reviewing and updating their risk management strategies to account for changes in the business environment or external factors.

By closely monitoring risks and taking proactive steps to mitigate them, the café shop not only managed to survive but also thrive in a competitive market. Over time, they expanded their business, opening new locations in other cities. The example here illustrates the significant impact that effective risk management can have on the growth and success of a small business.

4 Types of Monitoring

There are four key types of monitoring: *obligatory, voluntary, reassessment,* and *continual.* Obligatory monitoring is any assessment strategy required by law or regulation. Adhering to OSHA, FDA, or other industry regulations prompts obligatory monitoring to ensure everything is up-to-code. Voluntary monitoring is simply reviewing and watching company processes to learn and grow. These are any audits or tests your company runs to stay on track and be proactive. Reassessment monitoring applies specifically to your risk management processes. After any threats or problems, you'll reassess and review your procedures and strategies to refine them. Lastly, continual monitoring encompasses your everyday efforts to maintain awareness of your processes. These might include your Quality Assurance Systems, checklists, meetings, employee reviews, and any lines of communication and order to ensure transparency. By monitoring risks, a potentially fatal fall for your company can instead become a learning curve that empowers growth.

Risk Management: A Catalyst to Growth

As a risk consultant, my work with my clients is built on five pillars: Communication, Strategic, Futuristic, Competition, and Deliberative. Each of these pillars is ingrained into each of the five steps of the management process. In identifying risks, we must take a futuristic approach, exploring our goals and our "what-ifs." This is the *foundation* of growth. In analyzing risks, we must be deliberative, assessing every situation and event with a microscopic and competitive lens. This is where we begin to take the fear out of the unknown and carve out our own opportunities. In evaluating risks, we must be strategic. When we understand what's in our way, we can acquire the tools and talents needed to clear the path ahead of us. In controlling and monitoring risks, we must communicate. The health of your business communication reflects the longevity of your business. Overcoming conflict requires great communication — as we work together, we can rise above the risks and turn them into lessons that lead to our reward.

A successful business owner knows that risk management is a way to help grow the company and make it more stable. But it isn't just an important part of running your business — it also teaches you about yourself as a founder, leader, and individual. You can learn so much about yourself and your business when you start to look at the risks that you're facing and, in the process, discover opportunities to turn your vision into reality.

You understand that the first step in the process of growing your small business is to map out your path. You need to make sure that you have a strong understanding of what you want to accomplish and how you're going to get there. As you identify the risks and obstacles in your journey, prepare for the worst-case scenario, get to know your risk stakeholders, and overcome obstacles by evaluating risks, you can begin to make powerful decisions. As you harness the power of internal research and external research in the form of a guide, you can apply the best practices, expand your risk management toolkit, and, finally, grow forward. Growth isn't just an action — it's an intention. As we prepare for the future, we frame our success and strengthen our mindsets to believe there *is* a future. Confidence is a byproduct of preparedness. The clearer we can envision the future, the more deliberate, confident, and strategic our decisions will be. Fear lies in resisting the unknown — but confidence lies in embracing it. It's our adaptation and flexibility toward change that allows us to turn weaknesses into strengths and threats into opportunities. And as we look forward, we grow forward.

Please visit **www.rhysli.co** for more information on how Rhys can help and to schedule a free consulting session to identify risks in your business. For free resources and how I can help, **visit www.rhysli.co/SWOTanalysis** and **www.rhysli.co/riskstakeholderstemplate**.

Bibliography

"10 Business Continuity Stats to Make You Change for the Better." *SysGroup*. SysGroup Marketing. Accessed September 1, 2022. https://www.sysgroup.com/resources/blog/business-continuity-to-make-you-change-for-the-better.

"Beat the Statistics-the Reality of Risk Management." *Safran*. Safran Software Solutions, July 8, 2015. https://www.safran.com/blog/reality-of-risk-management.

"Best Practice Principles for Undertaking Risk Management." *myBUSINESS*. Accessed September 1, 2022. https://www.mybusiness.com.au/how-we-help/be-a-better-employer/managing-risk/best-practice-principles-for-undertaking-risk-management-on-your-business.

Christian, E. Forrest. "SP/A Theory and Operational Risk." *The Manasclerk Company*. Accessed September 1, 2022. http://www.manasclerk.com/blog/2021/03/30/sp-a-theory-and-operational-risk/.

Deb, Anirban, Suman Bhattacharya, Jeremy Gu, Tianxia Zhou, Eva Feng, and Mandie Liu. "Under the Hood of Uber's Experimentation Platform." *Uber Blog*, August 28, 2018. https://www.uber.com/blog/xp/.

Dweck, Carol. "What Having a 'Growth Mindset' Actually Means." *Harvard Business Review*, January 13, 2016. https://hbr.org/2016/01/what-having-a-growth-mindset-actually-means.

Gonzalez, Zarina. "Qualitative Risk Analysis & Quantitative Risk Analysis." *SafetyCulture*, August 3, 2022. https://safetyculture.com/topics/qualitative-and-quantitative-risk-analysis/.

Götting, Marie Charlotte. "Spotify: Number of Premium Subscribers Worldwide 2022." *Statista*, August 17, 2022. https://www.statista.com/statistics/244995/number-of-paying-spotify-subscribers/.

Insureon Staff. "Poll: 3 out of 4 Small Business Owners Consider Themselves Risk-Takers." *Insureon*, September 1, 2018. https://www.insureon.com/blog/small-business-owners-consider-themselves-risk-takers.

Insureon Staff. "What Is Risk Avoidance in Business Insurance?" What Is Risk Avoidance in Business Insurance? | *Insureon*, August 2, 2022. https://www.insureon.com/blog/what-is-risk-avoidance.

Kenton, Will, and Ryan Eichler. "Business Risk." Edited by Julius Mansa. *Investopedia,* March 25, 2022. https://www.investopedia.com/terms/b/businessrisk.asp.

Landes, Austin. "What Is a Risk Management Consultant?" *Landes Blosch*, September 12, 2019. https://www.landesblosch.com/blog/what-is-a-risk-management-consultant/.

Mitter, Christine, Kuttner, Michael, and Berchtenbreiter, Andreas. "Risk Management in a Small Family-Owned Nursery: A Case Study Approach." *Journal of the International Council for Small Business* 3, no. 1 (2022): 36-42. https://doi.org/10.1080/26437015.2021.1944790.

Nowak, Joan. "Case Study - Cleaning Service ." *Hybrid Business Advisors*, February 10, 2019. https://www.hybridbizadvisors.com/case-study/cleaning-service/.

Pimco. "Understanding the Risk/Reward Spectrum." *Pacific Investment Management Company LLC*. PIMCO. Accessed September 1, 2022. https://www.pimco.com/en-us/resources/education/stepping-up-the-risk-reward-spectrum/.

"Risk Management." *NI Business Info*. Accessed September 1, 2022. https://www.nibusinessinfo.co.uk/content/strategies-help-you-manage-business-risk.

"Root Cause Analysis Explained: Definition, Examples, and Methods." *Tableau*. Accessed September 1, 2022. https://www.tableau.com/learn/articles/root-cause-analysis.

Shefrin, Hersh. *Behavioral Risk Management: Managing the Psychology That Drives Decisions and Influences Operational Risk.* New York: Palgrave Macmillan US, 2016.

Sonnemaker, Tyler. "Airbnb Is Worth More than the 3 Largest Hotel Chains Combined after Its Stock Popped 143% on Its First Day of Trading." *Business Insider*, December 11, 2020. https://www.businessinsider.com/airbnb-ipo-valuation-tops-three-hotel-chains-combined-opening-day-2020-12.

Spud, Barry. "An Example of a Risk Management Plan for Use on Any Project." *Safety Risk*, March 18, 2014. https://safetyrisk.net/an-example-of-a-risk-management-plan-for-use-on-any-project/.

"SWOT Analysis Case Studies." SWOT analysis case studies. *Visual Paradigm Online*. Accessed September 1, 2022. https://online.visual-paradigm.com/knowledge/swot-analysis/swot-analysis-case-studies/.

Thapaliya, Sujan. "6 Brilliant Case Study Examples for Small Businesses." *SocialPilot*. Accessed September 1, 2022. https://www.socialpilot.co/blog/case-study-examples.

Thomas, Christine. "Five Steps of the Risk Management Process." *360factors*, January 20, 2022. https://www.360factors.com/blog/five-steps-of-risk-management-process/.

Wasserman, Noam. *The Founder's Dilemmas: Anticipating and Avoiding the Pitfalls That Can Sink a Startup.* New Jersey: Princeton University Press, 2012.

Westland, Jason. "The Best Risk Management Tools & Techniques for PM Pros." *ProjectManager*, July 7, 2022. https://www.projectmanager.com/blog/risk-management-tools-techniques.

Woods, Samuel J. "29 Growth Marketing Case Studies." *Stimulead*, April 25, 2022. https://stimulead.com/growth-marketing-case-studies/.

Yohn, Denise Lee. "How Airbnb Survived The Pandemic—And How You Can Too." *Forbes*, November 10, 2020.

About the Author

Having grown up in New York City, I understand risks both in personal and professional life. After graduation from university, I worked as an investigative auditor investigating white-collar crimes within New York City. After working as an investigator for several years, I moved to Big 4 consulting firms where I had the opportunity to manage international teams in assessing risks in the corporate world.

I am a Consultant, MBA, and a Risk Coach based in Amsterdam. Leveraging over 20 years of industry experience in risk consulting and finance, I help businesses, start-ups and newly established small businesses, and individuals improve processes, implement strategic systems, and increase productivity while reducing risk. I have an extensive experience working for both U.S. and Dutch companies in the financial sector, consumer products, technology, telecommunications, as well as oil and gas companies. Holding an unparalleled sense of leadership, I empower my clients to overcome challenges and barriers with confidence using his proprietary coaching method.

What do I know about entrepreneurship? As a son of a busy entrepreneur who never took vacations, and I deeply understand the impact that has on a family. Busy entrepreneurs seldom take time to relax and enjoy quality time with loved ones, often resulting in burnout and loss of business. My one-of-a-kind personal and business development coaching method brings balance and peace of mind back into the equation with strategic planning and risk assessment.

> *"I think coaching and consulting can guide business owners like my mom to reduce stress, enjoy life a bit more and have more valuable time with family. Having your own business doesn't necessarily mean freedom, without the right tools and mindset."*
>
> *– Rhys Li*

Through proof of concept, dedication to innovation, and unwavering commitment to helping clients thrive in the digital age, my **purpose-driven vision has come to fruition.**

www.ingramcontent.com/pod-product-compliance
Lightning Source LLC
Chambersburg PA
CBHW070442130626
46553CB00006B/2278